DOMINIC WOOD

simply MAGIC

RED FOX

Dedicated to my mum and dad and my three big brothers, who have given me the most amazing amount of support over the years!

Thanks to Michelle Worthington, Nigel Pope, Mark Leveridge, Neil Roberts, George Blake, Angelo Carbone, Roger Barrons, Ron Heaver, Garry Jones, Brian Doderidge, Philip Hitchcock, Richard McCourt, Duncan Trillo, Anthony Owen, Chris Pilkington, Paul Smith, Exonian Magical Society, The Magic Circle, but most of all to Sam Anstis-Brown for getting me started.

A Red Fox Book

Published by Random House Children's Books
20 Vauxhall Bridge Road, London SW1V 2SA

A division of The Random House Group Ltd
London Melbourne Sydney Auckland
Johannesburg and agencies throughout the world

Copyright © Dominic Wood 2000

1 3 5 7 9 10 8 6 4 2

First published by The Bodley Head Children's Books 2000

This edition 2001

Printed in Singapore by Tien Wah Press (PTE) Ltd

Papers used by The Random House Group Limited are natural, recyclable products made from wood grown in sustainable forest. The manufacturing processes conform to the environmental regulations of the country of origin.

THE RANDOM HOUSE GROUP Limited Reg. No. 954009

www.randomhouse.co.uk

ISBN 0 09 941396 5

Check out the star rating to see how difficult the trick is to learn or perform:

 easy

 moderate

 difficult

 very difficult

CONTENTS

INTRODUCTION

Hello! Welcome to the weird and wonderful world of magic, one of the oldest and most popular forms of entertainment.

I first got hooked on magic when my drumming teacher, Sam Anstis-Brown, made one of his drumsticks vanish. I remember seeing it simply disappear into thin air and I didn't have a clue where it had gone. I tried looking on the floor, up his sleeves, everywhere, but I couldn't find it! It wasn't until about three days later that he told me how he'd done it.

After I learnt that trick I bought some magic books and put on shows for my mum and dad and their friends. I would always practise my new tricks on my three big brothers. I think it used to drive them round the twist so, to get me back, they would take my books and learn my secrets, so make sure you find somewhere to keep this book safe from prying eyes.

Now I perform magic on TV. You may have seen me perform some of the tricks in this book. They look really amazing, but you'll be surprised how simple they are to learn and how easy they are to perform. Very soon you'll have your audience scratching their heads and wondering how the tricks were done. Who knows, one day you might even be performing magic on TV!

Anyway, enough yapping from me, let's get going. Good luck with your journey into magic, but most important of all – enjoy it!

Dominic Wood

THE RULES OF MAGIC

If you want to become a successful magician, the first thing you must do is spend some time learning the tricks of the trade. Pay attention to these five rules, and you will be off to a great start!

1 Ssh! Keep it a secret…

This is the most important rule of all, which is why it is the first rule. If you tell people how a trick is done, then you will not only spoil it for yourself, but also for your audience. They may tell you that they want to know the secret, but this is because people love the unexplained. So let's leave magic… unexplained!

2 Practise, practise, practise…

Remember, never perform a trick straight after you have learned it. I know you may be very excited and want to show off your hard work, but it is important to practise as much as possible. You will do your tricks without any hiccups and your audience will find it much more difficult to work out how it's done.

3 Do not repeat it….

Never repeat the same trick to the same audience at the same time or the same place. A trick that is performed a second time is never quite so impressive, and your audience will watch you more closely and may work out the secret to how it is done.

4 The right moment…

Magic is great when it is done at the right time and in the right place. If you perform magic tricks to your family and friends all the time, they will end up hating it.

5 Short and sweet…

It is far better to do a short magic show and leave your audience wanting more rather than doing a two-hour show and making your audience bored.

Every magician needs a magic wand to cast spells and perform their tricks successfully, so the next step to becoming a proper magician is to get hold of one of these. You can buy a wand from a toy store, but it is much more fun to make one yourself. Here are a couple of ways how:

PAPER WAND

WHAT YOU NEED
- A piece of black paper
- A piece of white paper
- A long pencil
- Glue

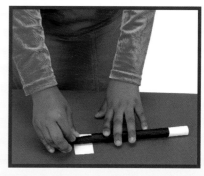

3 Leave the tube to dry and then glue a short piece of white paper around each end.

I Cut the black paper so it is slightly longer than the pencil, and about 5 cm wide.

2 Wrap the black paper around the pencil. Spread glue evenly along the edge of the paper and stick it down to form a tube.

4 Finally, slide out the pencil and, as if by magic, you now have a magic wand!

WOODEN WAND

WHAT YOU NEED
- A wooden cane (approx 30 cm long)
- Black paint
- White paint

1 Take the piece of wood and paint it black.

2 When it is dry, paint a white band roughly 3 cm long at each end and let it dry again. This wand is much more solid and will last a lot longer than the paper one.

★ STAR TIPS ★

When you are painting or gluing, make sure that you lay down lots of old newspaper, just in case you spill any glue or paint on your best table.

A chopstick makes a good magic wand, especially if your magic has an oriental style or look. You can paint it black and white, or just leave it plain!

MAGIC WORDS

Real magicians use special magic words while they cast their spells. Although there are lots of famous magic words, you can say anything you like. It can be great fun inventing words and rhymes that will fit in with your show, but in case you can't think of any good ones right now, here are a few to get you started:

SIM SALA BIM!

ABRACADABRA!

HOCUS POCUS!

HEY, PRESTO!

GIBBLEDY, GOBBLEDY, GOOP!

IZZY WIZZY, LET'S GET BUSY!

SMELLY PYJAMAS!

★☆☆☆

ICE COOL MAGIC

A small amount of water is poured into a cup, a magic word is spoken and amazingly when the cup is tipped over all that falls out is an ice cube.

PREPARATION

Put some toilet paper in the bottom of the cup. Place the ice cube on top of the toilet paper.

PERFORMANCE

1 Show the cup to your audience, making sure they cannot see inside it.

3 Now breathe into the cup and explain to your audience that your breath will freeze the water. The reason for doing this is to allow time for the water to soak into the toilet paper.

2 Pour a small trickle of water from the bottle into the cup.

4 Tip the mouth of the cup towards you until it is upside down, and catch the ice cube as it falls out.

RUNAWAY STRAWS

This is a fun trick to perform when you are in a fast-food restaurant, or it can be done on your magic table. Two straws are placed parallel to each other on a table. A magic spell is cast over your finger and when it is placed between the two straws, they roll apart from each other. Spooky!

PERFORMANCE

1 Place the two straws parallel to each other on a smooth, flat table so that they are at least 5 cm apart.

2 Cast a magic spell over your first finger and tell your audience to watch the straws very closely. (If they are watching the straws, they will not notice what you are doing.)

3 Place your finger on the table in between the straws and secretly, quietly and softly, blow on your fingernail. Your breath will pass over your nail and off to the sides, pushing the straws apart at great speed.

ANTI-GRAVITY CUPS

This is a trick with no strings attached! Your magic powers make it look as if you can defy the laws of gravity. Two cups are placed upside down on a book. When the book is turned upside down, the cup stick to it.
WOW!

WHAT YOU NEED
- Two drawing pins
- A notebook with a hard cover
- Two plastic cups

PREPARATION

Open the notebook and push the two drawing pins through the cover so that the pins are sticking out the front. Make the distance between the pins the same width as your thumb.

PERFORMANCE

HEY PRESTO!

1 Hold the book face up with your thumb on top between the pins and your fingers on the bottom.

2 Now take one of the cups and place it mouth down on the cover of the book so that the rim of the cup is sandwiched between one of the pins and your thumb. Do the same with the other cup on the other side of your thumb.

3 Cast a magic spell, then slowly turn the book upside down. The cups will stick to the book.

4 Wave your hand above and below the book to prove there are no strings.

5 Ask a member of your audience to say 'Now' whenever they want. When they do, remove your thumb and let the plastic cups fall to the floor, but keep hold of the book.

 STAR TIPS
Take extra care when using drawing pins to make sure you don't pierce your thumb on the pins.

★★☆☆

SMARTY PANTS

Three tubes of Smarties are shaken in turn to show that two are empty and one is full. The tubes are mixed around and a member of your audience is asked to guess which tube has the Smarties in. But no matter which one they choose, they will always be wrong!

WHAT YOU NEED

- Four tubes of Smarties
- An elastic band
- A jacket or long-sleeved jumper

PREPARATION

1 Put on a jacket or a long-sleeved jumper.

2 Empty three tubes of all their Smarties and put them aside to share with your friends later.

3 Attach the fourth tube (still full of Smarties) to the inside of your right wrist with the elastic band and cover up the tube with the sleeve of your jacket or jumper. Make sure the end of this tube cannot be seen up your sleeve.

PERFORMANCE

1 Put the three empty tubes in a row on the table in front of you. Tell your audience that one of them is full.

2 Pick up two of the tubes with your left hand – when you shake them, they will sound empty (because they are!).

3 Now pick up the third tube with your right hand and shake it. The tube hidden up your sleeve will rattle and everyone will think that the tube you are shaking is full.

4 Ask a member of your audience to keep an eye on the full tube, while you mix the tubes around. Make sure that each time you pick up the tube that is meant to be full you do it with your right hand, so it rattles.

5 When you have mixed them around, ask your helper to point to the full tube. Whichever one is chosen, shake it with your left hand – it will sound empty!

★ STAR TIPS ★

You don't have to use tubes of Smarties. The trick works equally well if you fill a matchbox with beans or lentils, and have empty matchboxes on the table.

6 Now shake one of the other tubes with your right hand. This time it will rattle. You can repeat this trick – but don't do it too often or someone might work it out.

★★☆☆

WONDERFUL WAND

Magicians usually use magic wands to make magic happen, but in this trick the magic happens to the wand itself! A magic wand is placed inside a clear plastic bottle, whereupon it takes on a life of its own and starts to float inside the bottle with no visible means of support.

WHAT YOU NEED
- Blu-tack
- Very thin, black cotton
- A safety pin
- A magic wand
- A clear plastic bottle

PREPARATION

1 Cut off a 50 cm length of cotton. Attach a small amount of Blu-tack to one end and tie the other end to the safety pin.

2 Attach the safety pin to the inside of your jacket and stick the small piece of Blu-tack to one end of the wand.

PERFORMANCE

1 Turn the plastic bottle upside down to prove that it is empty. You could even sound a note by blowing across the top of it.

2 Now place the wand inside the bottle (Blu-tack side first).

3 Move the bottle away from your body. The wand will start to move up and down inside – it will look like it is floating. Make sure you do this at some distance from your audience, or in a dimly lit room, to make sure they don't see the cotton.

4 Once you have made the wand go up and down a few times, take it out and hand the bottle to your audience for examination. While they are looking at the bottle, secretly remove the Blu-tack from the wand. Then you can hand them the wand. If you wanted to be mean, you could ask them to try the trick out for themselves.

★ **STAR TIPS** ★

Once you have made the wand rise from the bottle, why not try the same trick, but have the wand rise from your hand instead. Try it, it really works!

★★☆☆

X-RAY EYES

Demonstrate your powerful **X-Ray** vision in this clever coin trick. Five coins are placed in a row on the table, and then you turn around. A member of your audience is asked to turn the coins over two at a time and then cover one with their hand. When you turn around, you immediately tell them whether the hidden coin is showing heads or tails.

WHAT YOU NEED
• Five coins

PERFORMANCE

1 Lay out the coins in front of you, making sure that they are all facing heads up.

3 When you turn back, look at the other coins. If there are an even number of heads showing, then the covered coin is heads. If there are an odd number of heads showing, then the covered coin is tails.

2 Now ask a member of your audience to turn the coins over two at a time while your back is turned and to slide one coin forward and cover it with their hand.

4 Once you have worked out what side the coin is, pretend you have X-Ray vision and that you will use your powers to look through their hand to see what the coin is. Tell them and watch their faces…

SNAPPY MATCH

A match is wrapped up in an empty handkerchief and a member of your audience is invited up to snap the match in half. A spell is cast... and the match is magically restored.

PREPARATION

Most cotton handkerchiefs have small openings in the seams at the corners. Find one in your handkerchief and push a match inside the seam so it is hidden.

PERFORMANCE

1 Lay the handkerchief flat on the table and place a match in the middle. Fold the four corners of the handkerchief into the middle, so that the match hidden in the seam lies next to the one you have just put there.

2 Invite a member of your audience to come up and snap the match. Hand them the handkerchief in such a way that you make sure they snap the hidden match, but of course they will think they are snapping the match they just saw you put in the handkerchief.

3 Now put the handkerchief back on the table. Say a few magic words and wave your wand. Everyone will be astonished when you open the handkerchief and reveal that the match is still in one piece.

NO BANG BALLOON

This trick will make your audience put their fingers in their ears, but they don't have to... well, unless it goes wrong! A fully inflated balloon appears to be normal, but once you cast a spell, it becomes indestructible. To prove this, you push a needle in one side and out the other, but the balloon doesn't pop.

WHAT YOU NEED
- A balloon
- Sticky tape
- A long needle
- Vaseline

PREPARATION

1 Blow up a balloon and put a small piece of sticky tape at the very top and the very bottom.

2 Rub some Vaseline on the needle to make it slide through the balloon more easily.

PERFORMANCE

1 Tell your audience that you will pop the balloon and it will make a very loud bang.

2 Now, with a steady hand, push the needle through the sticky tape at the top of the balloon. Because the tape is holding the balloon together, it won't pop! Keep pushing the needle until you reach the bottom, then push the needle out, through the other piece of sticky tape.

3 Finish the trick with a flourish. Pull out the needle and pop the balloon!

PENNY PUZZLE

This clever puzzle will offer a tricky challenge. A coin is balanced on a match over the opening of a bottle, and a helper is asked to make it fall in without touching the match, the bottle or the coin. When they have given up trying, you drip a few drops of water on the match, and the coin falls into the bottle. Easy!

> **WHAT YOU NEED**
> • A match
> • An empty bottle
> • A coin
> • A glass of water

PERFORMANCE

1 Take the match and snap it in half so that it forms a V shape, but make sure it is not completely broken.

2 Place the V-shaped match on top of the bottle. Carefully place the coin on top of the match so that it can fall straight down without hitting the edge of the opening.

3 Ask a member of your audience if they can think of a way to make the coin fall into the bottle without touching the coin, the match or the bottle, and without blowing. Unless they know the secret, they will not be able to.

4 When they have given up, simply dip your finger into the glass of water and allow a few drops of water to drip onto the broken part of the match. The match will begin to straighten, allowing the coin to fall into the bottle.

IS THIS YOUR CARD?

This easy card trick will make it look as if you have special mind-reading skills. A member of your audience is asked to choose a card from a pack of cards, remember it and then put it back. The pack is shuffled and then you look through the cards. Amazingly, you find the card that they chose.

WHAT YOU NEED
• A pack of cards

PREPARATION

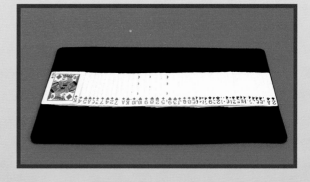

I You do not have to make anything special for this trick. Simply arrange the pack of cards so that all the black cards (Clubs and Spades) are at the bottom, and all the red cards (Hearts and Diamonds) are at the top.

PERFORMANCE

1 Ask a member of your audience to pick a card and remember what it is.

2 Ask your helper to put their card back, but to keep thinking about it so that their thought waves pass across to you. Offer them the pack so that they replace the card in the opposite half of the pack from where they picked it.

3 Square up the cards and put them on the table. Take a batch of cards from the top of the pack and put them beside the pack. Put the cards from the bottom of the pack on top of the cards on the table. This is called a cut.

4 Square up the cards and cut them again. Do this several times, and while you are cutting the cards, tell your audience that you are mixing them up. In fact, it doesn't matter how many times you do this, you will still be able to find the card they chose.

5 After you have cut the pack enough times to make your audience believe it is properly mixed up, look through the cards (making sure no one else sees the faces). There will be a card that is a different colour to all the other ones around it. This will be the card they chose. Whip it out with a flourish, and leave your audience amazed!

★★☆☆

JACK ATTACK!

Here's another card trick that's simple, but very effective. Three Jacks are taken out of a pack and shown to the audience. One is placed on top of the pack, one on the bottom and one in the middle. A helper is asked to cut the pack once to mix it around, the audience shouts 'Jack Attack!' and when your helper looks through the pack, they find all three Jacks in one place.

WHAT YOU NEED
• A pack of cards

PREPARATION

1 There is little to do for this trick, just make sure that one Jack is at the top of the pack.

PERFORMANCE

1 Look through the pack of cards and take out three Jacks, leaving the Jack you prepared earlier on the top. Show the Jacks quickly to your audience, so they don't get a chance to see what suits they are.

2 Now put one Jack on top of the pack, another Jack on the bottom and, finally, put the last Jack anywhere in the middle.

3 Place the cards on the table and invite a member of your audience to come up and cut the pack so that the bottom section of cards now lies on top. Even though cutting the pack gives the illusion of mixing the cards up, actually it is doing the opposite and bringing the Jacks together!

JACK ATTACK!

4 Ask your audience to shout 'Jack Attack!' and then ask your helper to look through the pack. They will find all three Jacks are now in the same place!

★ STAR TIPS ★

If you can find an identical pack of cards, you can do the same trick but with four Jacks, which is much better! Prepare the pack by putting the two spare Jacks on top. After you have found the four Jacks, put one Jack on the top and one on the bottom, but this time put two in the middle. And you know what to do next!

IT'S KNOT A PROBLEM

This knotty puzzle will amaze your friends, and when you show them how it's done, they'll all want to have a go. You take a piece of string and tie a knot in it without letting go of the ends, seemingly performing the impossible.

WHAT YOU NEED
- A piece of rope or string approx 1 metre long

PERFORMANCE

1 Challenge a member of your audience to tie a knot in the piece of string without letting go of the ends. No matter how hard they try, they won't be able to.

2 Once your helper has tried for some time and finally given up, lay the string in front of you.

3 Fold your arms like you are told to do at school when you've been naughty, and pick up an end of the string in each hand.

4 Now, without letting go of the ends of the string, uncross your arms. You will find that you have formed a knot. No problem!

VANISHING PENCIL

This was the first trick that I ever learned, and it made me want to start learning magic. A pencil is thrown as if it were a dart, but it vanishes into thin air. AMAZING!

PERFORMANCE

1 To start, you must be standing with your left side towards your audience. Hold the pencil by the writing end in front of you and level with your right ear.

3 Immediately bring your hand forward and pretend to throw the 'pencil', whereupon it vanishes.

2 Move the pencil backwards and forwards as if you were aiming a dart at a dartboard. On the third backward movement, slide the pencil behind your right ear and leave it there.

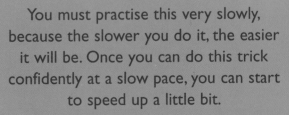

★ **STAR TIPS** ★
You must practise this very slowly, because the slower you do it, the easier it will be. Once you can do this trick confidently at a slow pace, you can start to speed up a little bit.

Make sure that you don't pause for too long while you are putting the pencil behind your ear.

FLASH CASH

This trick won't make you rich, but your friends will be handing you pieces of paper for the rest of your life. Four blank pieces of paper are shown on both sides and then folded into a small package. Amazingly, when the package is opened, the paper has changed into real money!

WHAT YOU NEED
- Four £5 notes
- Four pieces of paper (the same size as the £5 notes)
- Glue

PREPARATION

1 Holding all the paper together, fold the top third down and the bottom third up. Then fold the left and right thirds in, so that you end up with a small package. Now do the same with the £5 notes, and then stick the two packages together.

2 Once the glue has dried, keep the notes folded, but open the paper.

PERFORMANCE

1 Start by showing your audience the pieces of paper. Show both sides of three of the pieces, but when you show them the piece with the package on the back, cover it with your fingers.

3 When all the £5 notes are unfolded, show them to your audience in the same way you did the paper. There you go, money from nowhere. Imagine if you could do it for real. Wow!

2 Square the pieces of paper (keeping the package on the bottom), and fold them up. As you make the final fold, secretly turn the whole lot over and, without stopping, start to unfold the £5 notes.

> ★ **STAR TIPS** ★
>
> You don't have to get hold of real £5 notes to do this trick. It works equally well if you use Monopoly money or design your own notes.
>
> Use thin paper, otherwise it is difficult to make a neat bundle.
>
> As a little joke, you could write "I.O. U. £5" on each of the blank pieces of paper and pretend that a friend of yours owes you £20 and has given you these I.O.U.'s instead.

WHERE'S THE WATCH?

After you've performed this trick, everyone will think that time really can fly! A watch is borrowed from someone in your audience and covered with a handkerchief. Three people in the audience check that it is still under there, but when you shake out the handkerchief, the watch has vanished!

WHAT YOU NEED
- A clean handkerchief
- A secret helper

PREPARATION

I You do not need to make anything for this trick, but you do need to brief a stooge (a friend who is pretending to be a member of your audience, but is actually in on the trick). You will need to practise secretly passing the watch to them and discuss where you are going to make it appear from at the end of the trick.

PERFORMANCE

1 Ask someone in your audience if you can borrow their watch, and then cover it with your handkerchief.

2 Hold the watch through the handkerchief and ask another member of the audience to feel the watch by putting their hand underneath the handkerchief to check that it is still there.

3 Repeat step two with a second member of your audience.

★ **STAR TIPS** ★
Make sure your stooge looks surprised when you find the watch is on their wrist

4 Now ask the stooge to feel the watch, and while they are saying, 'Yes, it is still there,' secretly pass them the watch.

HEY PRESTO!

5 Pretend that you are still holding the watch and go back to the stage. Say some magic words and cast your magic wand, then throw the handkerchief into the air. The watch will have disappeared!

6 When the owner of the watch eventually asks for it back, go over to your stooge and point out that it is now on their wrist.

★★★☆

Magnetic Wand

This great trick will make your audience think that your magic wand really is magical! A wand is held in your hand, but when you open your fingers, instead of falling to the ground, it sticks to you as if you are magnetic.

WHAT YOU NEED
- A watch
- A pencil
- A magic wand

PREPARATION

1 Put on the watch and push one end of the pencil under the watch strap, so that it lies along the inside of your wrist. Position most of the pencil against the palm of your hand and make sure you keep it hidden from your audience. It is very important that they never see the pencil.

PERFORMANCE

1 Keeping the palm of the hand wearing the watch turned towards your body, place the centre of the magic wand in between the hidden pencil and the palm of your hand, so that the wand sticks out either side of your hand.

3 Slowly open the fingers of the hand holding the wand. The pressure of the pencil will keep the wand against your palm and from the front it will look like it's sticking to your hand.

4 After you have explained about your magnetic powers, close your fingers around the wand and remove it with your other hand. You can now let your audience examine the wand for any signs of 'stickiness'.

ABRACADABRA!

2 Close your fingers around the wand, so it looks as if you are holding it. Now pretend to sprinkle some invisible magic dust over your hand and wand, and say a magic word.

★ STAR TIPS ★

While your audience is examining the wand, casually place your hand in your pocket and leave the pencil behind.

Do not practise the trick too much or your wrist will get sore.

INVISIBLE CATCH

A stretch of the imagination is needed for this trick, but your audience will be amazed at the result.
A helper is told to throw an imaginary object towards an empty bag you are holding. Even though the object is invisible, it lands in the bag with a definite thud.

WHAT YOU NEED
• A paper bag

PERFORMANCE

I Hold the paper bag in between your second finger and thumb so that your thumb is on the outside of the bag.

2 Ask a member of your audience to imagine that they are holding an object in their hand and to throw it into the paper bag.

3 As they throw the 'object' towards the bag, snap your finger and thumb together as if you were clicking your fingers. If you do it correctly, this will 'jolt' the bag and it will look and sound as if something has landed inside.

★ STAR TIPS ★
Even though this is more of a joke, you can turn it into a trick by placing a boiled sweet in the bag at the beginning. After you have made the bag jolt, look inside with amazement and take out the sweet, which you then give to your helper.

GLASS GO

Your audience is told that you are going to make a coin disappear by covering it with a tumbler and wrapping the tumbler in paper. However, the tumbler vanishes instead of the coin. Much more impressive!

PERFORMANCE

1 Sit behind a table that is covered with a cloth and place the coin on the table. Tell your audience that you are going to make the coin disappear but to do so you will need to cover it up.

4 While you pretend to be upset that the coin hasn't vanished, secretly let the glass fall into your lap. This should be done below the level of the table. Even though there is nothing there, the paper will still hold the shape of the glass.

2 Place the tumbler, mouth down, over the coin. Then wrap the sheet of newspaper around it.

3 Mutter a few magic words and lift the covered glass towards your lap. At this point, your audience will see that the coin is still there, so you should look disappointed.

5 Tell your audience that you have failed to make the coin disappear, so you will do another trick instead. At this point, open up the paper and amaze everyone!

Pick 'n' Predict

In this card trick you cunningly make a member of your audience choose the card that you want them to. After they have selected a card from the pack, you take out a piece of paper from a sealed envelope to reveal the name of the card printed on it. Impossible, but true!

WHAT YOU NEED
- Paper
- A pen
- A pack of cards
- An envelope

PREPARATION

1 Write YOU WILL PICK THE FIVE OF CLUBS on a piece of paper and seal it inside the envelope.

2 Before you start the trick, place the Five of Clubs face down on top of the pack of cards.

PERFORMANCE

1 Ask a member of your audience to come up and help you. Tell them that inside the envelope is the name of the playing card that you think they will choose.

2 Pick up the pack of cards and ask your helper to lift off a quarter of the cards, turn them face up and place them back on top of the remainder of the pack.

4 Now fan out the cards from left to right from the top and ask your helper to remove the first face-down card they see. They will not know it yet but they have taken the Five of Clubs, which you secretly placed on top of the pack before you started the trick.

3 Now ask them to lift off half the cards (including the reversed ones on top), turn them over and again place them back on top of the remainder of the pack.

5 Ask your helper to show the card to the rest of your audience and then open the envelope to read the prediction. Of course, it will be correct!

★★★☆

Linking Mints

This simple trick can be done with props you could pull out of your pocket. Two Polo mints are put into an empty matchbox. A magic spell is cast, and when they are tipped out, they have magically become linked together. **WOW!**

PREPARATION

1 Stick the small piece of card in the middle of the empty matchbox, so that the tray is divided into two equal-sized compartments.

WHAT YOU NEED
- A small piece of card (approx 1 cm by 3 cm)
- An empty matchbox
- Glue
- A packet of Polo mints

2 Snap a Polo mint in half and place one of the halves through the hole of another mint. Lick the broken end of one half and join it to its other half. Press quite hard and wait for it to dry. When it is dry, you should end up with what looks like two linked Polo mints.

3 Put the linked mints into one side of the matchbox tray and slide the matchbox sleeve back on.

PERFORMANCE

1 Take two mints from the packet and place them in the empty half of the matchbox. Close the box and place it on the table.

3 Pick up the matchbox and carefully slide it halfway open to reveal the half with the linked mints in. Then, Hey Presto, carefully tip out the two linked mints!

2 Cast a spell with some magic words and wave your wand over the matchbox.

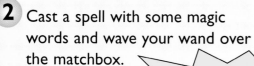

HEY PRESTO!

★ STAR TIPS ★

If there are any matches in the matchbox, ask an adult to take them out and keep them safe for you.

Cover the matchbox in bright paper or foil to make it look more special.

★★★★

THE KEY TO MAGIC

A lot of people ask me what the key to magic is, well when you've done this trick you'll see! A key is shown to the audience, covered with a handkerchief and, in a flash, completely disappears!

PREPARATION

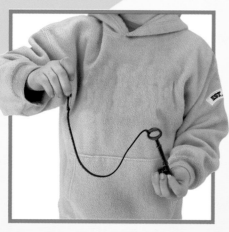

WHAT YOU NEED
- A key
- A piece of elastic (approx 30 cm long)
- A safety pin
- A handkerchief
- You also need to be wearing a jacket

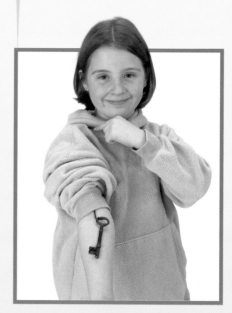

1 Thread one end of the elastic through the hole in the key and tie it on. Tie the other end to the safety pin.

2 Attach the safety pin to the inside of your jacket sleeve at the top, so the elastic runs down your sleeve.

3 The key should hang just below your elbow. Just before you perform the trick, pull the key down your sleeve and secretly hold it in your hand.

PERFORMANCE

1 Tell your audience that you have found the key to magic and open your hand to show them the key. This should get a little laugh!

2 Now cover the key with the handkerchief. When the key is hidden, let go of it and the elastic will make it fly up your sleeve.

3 Once it is safely up your sleeve, remove the handkerchief – the key will have vanished!

DOUBLE YOUR MONEY

If you don't think you get enough pocket money, then try this trick. A 20 pence coin is dropped into an empty matchbox, which is then closed. When the matchbox is opened again, the coin has become a 50 pence piece.

PREPARATION

1 Take the knife and carefully cut a small slot in the end of the tray. It should be just big enough for the 20 pence coin to slide out but small enough to keep the 50 pence coin in. Ask an adult to help you do this.

2 Now position the tray so it is halfway inside the matchbox sleeve, and sandwich the 50 pence coin in between the tray and the top of the sleeve.

PERFORMANCE

I Take out the matchbox that you prepared earlier. Explain to your audience that coins can grow just like humans and drop the 20 pence coin into the tray. Then tip the matchbox back to let the coin secretly slide out of the slot into your hand.

2 Now close the box. As you do this, the 50 pence coin will fall into the tray. Shake the box so that the coin can be heard rattling inside.

ABRACADABRA!

3 Say a magic word, then open the box to reveal the 50 pence coin!

★ STAR TIPS ★

When the 50 pence coin is loose inside the box, take out a magic wand from your pocket leaving the 20 pence coin behind. This way you will not have to hide the 20 pence coin in your hand for the whole of your trick.

You can do this trick with other combinations of coins. Just make sure that the one left in the box is bigger than the one that you are going to tip out.

★★★★

Indestructible String

A piece of string is threaded through a drinking straw and the straw is cut in half. Mysteriously, even though the straw is now in two halves, the string remains in one piece.

WHAT YOU NEED
- A drinking straw
- A piece of string which is at least 10 cm longer than the straw
- Scissors

PREPARATION

1 Prepare your straw by making a 5 cm long slit down its middle.

PERFORMANCE

1 Thread the string through the straw and fold the straw in half.

2 Hold the straw roughly 3 cm from the folded point between the fingers of one hand.

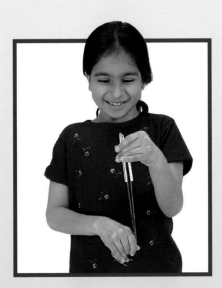

3 With your other hand, secretly pull the ends of the string downwards. This will bring the centre of the string down the slit and away from the folded point.

4 Now, very carefully, cut the straw in half where it has been folded. Your audience will believe that you have cut the string as well as the straw.

5 Take one half of the straw in each hand and pull your hands apart. The straw is clearly in two halves, but magically the string is still intact.

★ **STAR TIPS** ★
To make it more of a mystery, you could get a helper to cut the straw in half, but you must tell them to be careful, otherwise they could cut you.

CRAFTY CARD

You need to have nimble fingers to perform this trick successfully, but once you have mastered the movement, it will look very impressive. The Jack of Hearts is produced and covered with a handkerchief. A magic spell is cast over the card and when the handkerchief is removed, the card has changed into the Queen of Clubs.

WHAT YOU NEED
- The Jack of Hearts
- The Queen of Clubs
- Glue
- Another playing card
- A clean handkerchief

PREPARATION

1 Take the Jack and fold it exactly in half (face inwards). Fold the Queen in the same way.

2 Now put some glue on the back of one half of both cards. Stick the glued halves of the Jack and the Queen together, so they are back to back.

3 Put some glue on the face of the extra card and stick it to the back of the remaining halves of the Jack and the Queen.

4 Once the glue has dried, you will end up with a special card, which has a flap in the centre. When it is folded one way, it will show the Jack. When it is folded the other way, it will show the Queen.

PERFORMANCE

1 Take the special flap card and hold the flap down so it looks like an ordinary Jack of Hearts. Show both sides of the card to your audience.

3 Cast a spell with your wand and say a magic word. Remove the handkerchief and show both sides of the card to your audience. They will be astonished to see you are now holding the Queen of Clubs.

2 Now cover the card with a handkerchief. As you do so, flip the flap the other way to change the card into the Queen of Clubs, and hold it closed.

★ STAR TIPS ★

Once you have perfected the 'flap' move under the handkerchief, try and change the Jack to a Queen by just moving your hand over the card. If you practise hard, it will look very impressive!

PUTTING ON A MAGIC SHOW

After lots of practice and preparation you will be ready to put on a magic show. But making sure you do all the tricks successfully isn't the only thing you have to think about. It's also important to be wearing the right clothes, saying the right things and making sure the stage is right. Here are a few handy hints to make sure your show's a spectacular success!

Practising for a Show
You can practise for a magic show in several ways. If you stand in front of a full-length mirror, you will see the trick as your audience will see it. You can also practise in front of a video camera, if you have one. The good thing about doing this is that you can play back the video and watch what areas need improvement and also what looked good. However, the best kind of practice is actually performing in front of an audience. The more you perform, the more you will learn and the better you will get.

Looking the Part
It has been traditional for magicians to wear a top hat and tails for the last two hundred years. However, things have changed and not all magicians look like this any more. It's quite useful to wear a jacket – the pockets are handy to put props in and you can hide tricks up the sleeves – but wearing items that make you look unique will make sure you and your act stand out.

Setting the Stage

An imaginative and dramatic stage will create a great impression, but there are some things that all sets should have. If you are using lots of different props, it is useful to have a table to put them on, and there are lots of tricks that need to be performed on a table. You can make a normal table look magical by covering it with a cloth, and then decorating it with a crystal ball or some candles.

How to Handle Your Audience

You need to think about where to position your audience. Most of the audience should be directly in front of you, but some may sit slightly to one side. This is OK, but be careful – if they sit too far round to the side, they might see how some tricks are done.

When you invite a member of the audience to help you with a trick, always choose your helper carefully! Don't choose anyone who likes to be centre of

attention – they might upstage you and ruin your show.

When someone is helping you with a trick, always treat them with respect. There's a difference between having fun and making fun!

A Star Performance

Start your show by introducing yourself and then kick off with a trick that is quick and to the point to establish that you are a magician. Never include a member of your audience in the first or last trick.

Patter, or what you say, is very important. It acts as a distraction when you want your audience to look away from your hands, and a trick is more interesting if you have a story to go with it.

Tommy Cooper used to tell jokes while doing his magic. You can do the same – look in a joke book and put some jokes into your act. However, if you are not a confident speaker, you can perform your magic to music. I used to do this a lot when I started performing. When you pick your music, you should choose something that helps create a magical atmosphere – not heavy metal!

FURTHER MAGIC

When you can do all the tricks in this book, you will be off to a great start in becoming a magician. But what should you do next? Firstly, you must practise as much as you can. You also need to learn new magic tricks, to keep your shows full of surprises. If you are really serious, you could join a magical society, to learn their secrets and meet more young magicians.

New Magic Tricks

As well as learning tricks from magic books, you can also buy tricks from special magic shops. Lots of shops have catalogues, so you can have a good look before you choose the tricks you want. When you are starting out, it is a good idea to ask them to recommend some simple tricks. Here are just some of the places you could try:

International Magic
89 Clerkenwell Road
London EC1R 5BX
Tel: 020 7405 7324

Mark Leveridge Magic
13A Lyndhurst Road
Exeter
Devon
EX2 4PA
Tel: 01392 252000
Or check out their web site:
www.markleveridge.co.uk

Davenports Magic
7 Charing Cross
Underground Shopping Arcade
The Strand
London WC2N 4HZ
Tel: 020 7836 0408

Magical Societies

There are many magical societies around Britain, but the leading society for young magicians is The Young Magicians Club. They have regular meetings and a regular newsletter is also sent out. You can visit their web site at:
www.youngmagiciansclub.co.uk
but if you don't have access to a computer, you can write for more information to:
The Young Magicians Club
The Magic Circle HQ
12 Stephenson Way
London NW1 2HD